Imam Abbas
Mosque In
Karbala

FACES
AND
PLACES

IRAQ

LARAMIE JUNIOR HIGH SCHOOL
1355 North 22nd
Laramie, WY 82072

BY KATHRYN STEVENS

THE CHILD'S WORLD®, INC.

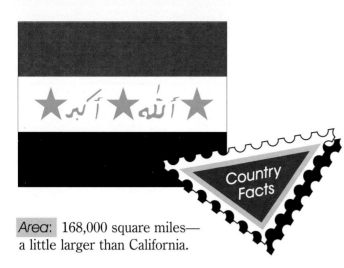

Country Facts

Area: 168,000 square miles— a little larger than California.

Population: About 20 million people.

Capital City: Baghdad.

Other Important Cities: Al Basrah, Mosul, Karkuk, and Arbil.

Important Rivers: The Tigris and Euphrates.

Money: The dinar (dih–NAR). One dinar is made up of 1,000 fils.

National Flag: A flag with a red stripe across the top, a white stripe across the middle, and a black stripe across the bottom. The white stripe has three green stars and Arabic letters that spell out "God is Almighty."

National Song: "Al-Salaam al Jumhuri," or "Salute of the Republic."

Official Name: The Republic of Iraq (Al-Jumhariya Al-Iraqiya).

Head of Government: The president of Iraq.

Library of Congress Cataloging-in-Publication Data
Stevens, Kathryn, 1954-
Iraq / by Kathryn Stevens.
Series: "Faces and Places".
p. cm.
Includes index.
Summary: An introduction to the history, geography, people and customs of the Republic of Iraq.
ISBN 1-56766-580-2 (library : reinforced : alk. paper)

1. Iraq — Juvenile literature.
[1. Iraq] I. Title.

DS70.6.S84 1999
956.7 — dc21
98-44249
CIP
AC

GRAPHIC DESIGN
Robert A. Honey, Seattle

PHOTO RESEARCH
James R. Rothaus / James R. Rothaus & Associates

ELECTRONIC PRE–PRESS PRODUCTION
Robert E. Bonaker / Graphic Design & Consulting Co.

PHOTOGRAPHY
Cover photo: Iraqi Girls in Traditional Costume by Francoise de Mulder/Corbis

Table
of
Contents

CHAPTER	PAGE

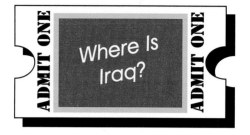

Where Is Iraq?

If you looked at Earth from high above, what would you see? You would see huge land areas surrounded by water. These land areas are called **continents**. Iraq lies at the southwestern edge of a large continent called Asia.

Western Hemisphere

Eastern Hemisphere

Iraq (white) is in the east and U.S.A. (green) is in the west

Iraq is surrounded by several other countries —Iran, Turkey, Syria, Jordan, Saudi Arabia, and tiny Kuwait. These countries are part of a region called the Middle East.

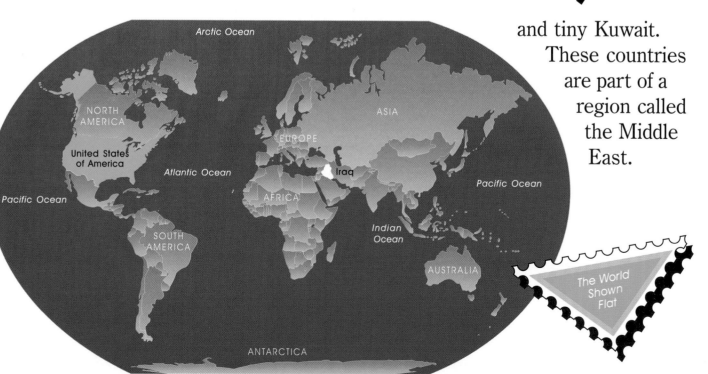

Arctic Ocean

NORTH AMERICA

United States of America

Atlantic Ocean

Pacific Ocean

ASIA

EUROPE

Iraq

AFRICA

Pacific Ocean

Indian Ocean

SOUTH AMERICA

AUSTRALIA

ANTARCTICA

The World Shown Flat

TURKEY

SYRIA

IRAN

IRAQ

JORDAN

SAUDI
ARABIA

KUWAIT

*Persian
Gulf*

Marsh With
Canoes
Near
An Nasiriyah

Hajj Umran

Euphrates River

Tigris River

DESERT

Khan El Baghdadi

Karbala

Uruk

An Nasiriyah

PERSIAN GULF

Nik Wheeler/Corbis

The Land

Most of Iraq is hot and dry. In fact, it gets only a few inches of rain each year. Few people live in the dry, rocky desert of western Iraq. The northern hills, mountains, and valleys are not as dry. Iraq's two large rivers are the Tigris and Euphrates (yoo–FRAY–tees). They flow through central Iraq toward the Persian Gulf. The rivers supply much-needed water for drinking and farming. Near the Persian Gulf is a region of large marshes.

Some parts of Iraq have huge, underground oil fields. The Middle East's oil is used throughout the world. It is used for making gasoline and other fuels, plastics, and countless other products.

Euphrates River Near Khan El Baghdadi

Nik Wheeler/Corbis

Sumerian Ruins And Desert At Uruk

Hajj Umran In Northern Iraq

Nik Wheeler/Corbis

Nik Wheeler/Corbis

Plants & Animals

ADMIT ONE • ADMIT ONE

Nik Wheeler/Corbis

Camels Drinking Near Ukhaidir

Most of Iraq is too hot and dry for many plants. Grasses and shrubs grow in some regions. Trees such as willow and poplar live in some of the valleys. One of Iraq's most valuable plants is the *date palm*. Date palms produce sweet, tasty dates that the Iraqis eat or sell to other countries. Iraq's food crops include wheat and barley. The crops are grown by pumping river water onto the dry fields. This kind of watering is called **irrigation**.

Iraq has much less wildlife than it did long ago. A small, horned antelope called a *gazelle* still runs free. So do some wild pigs, foxes, wolves, and hyenas.

Lizards and snakes creep along the ground even in the dry deserts. Birds such as storks, hawks and vultures soar across the sky. The marshes are home to ducks and geese.

Date Palms And Ruins On Raya Island

Man With Falcon In Al Basrah

Charles & Josette Lenars/Corbis

Nik Wheeler/Corbis

RAYA ISLAND

Ukhaidir

An Nasiriyah

Al Basrah

Wild Boars
Running
Through
Marsh Near
An Nasiriyah

Babylon
Gate In
Mesopotamia

Hatra ∴

■ *ASSYRIAN SCULPTURE*

Babylon ∴
MESOPOTAMIA

Ur ∴

Long Ago

Ruins Of 1st Century A.D. City Of Hatra

Nik Wheeler/Corbis

Early humans lived in Iraq more than 100,000 years ago! Much later, the Greeks called central Iraq **Mesopotamia**, or "the land between the rivers." Mesopotamia's people were some of the first farmers in the world. Over 10,000 years ago, they tamed, or **domesticated**, wheat and barley and grew them for food. They domesticated animals, too, and raised them for their meat, milk, and hides. These animals included goats, sheep, pigs, donkeys, cattle, and horses.

Slowly, Mesopotamia's people changed their way of life. They stopped roaming around, hunting wild foods, and camping in different spots. Instead, they spent more time in one place. Villages grew into cities, and then into larger kingdoms. Iraq's Sumerian, Assyrian, and Babylonian kingdoms were each very important in shaping world history.

Ruins Of Ancient City Of Ur, Iraq

9th Century B.C. Assyrian Sculpture

Gianni Dagli Orti/Corbis

David Lees/©Corbis

Iraq
Today

Iraqi Soldiers Fighting Iran At Khorramshahr

Francoise de Mulder/Corbis

Iraq has been ruled by many different kings and emperors. In 1958, military leaders overthrew the king and created a new government. The new leaders often plotted against each other. One of them, Saddam Hussein (sah–dahm hoo–SANE) became president in 1979. He has ruled ever since, arresting and even killing people who oppose him—including members of his own family. Rulers who have total power over their people are called **dictators.**

The past 20 years have been difficult for the Iraqi people. An eight-year war with Iran killed hundreds of thousands of people. In 1990, Iraq took over another neighboring country, Kuwait. The United States, Saudi Arabia, and other nations took back Kuwait in a short but intense war called the Gulf War. This war killed thousands more Iraqis and wrecked buildings, roads, and bridges. Today, Iraq's relations with the United States and many other countries are still very tense. Almost no Americans ever travel to Iraq.

King Faisal II Of Iraq, 1956

UPI/Corbis-Bettmann

Kurds Fled From Hussein To A Refugee Camp Near Zakho

U.S. Department of Defense/Corbis

14

Zakho

Baghdad ☆

IRAN

SAUDI ARABIA

Khorramshahr
PERSIAN GULF
KUWAIT

Portrait Of
Saddam
Hussein
In Baghdad

The Great
Shiite
Mosque In
Baghdad

TURKEY

☆ Baghdad

Karbala•

• An Nasiriyah

Roger Wood/©Corbis

The People

Arab Father And Daughter Near An Nasiriyah

Nik Wheeler/Corbis

Iraqi people are very family-oriented. Most of them are *Arabs*. They are also *Muslims*, or followers of the Islamic religion. Iraq has two groups of Muslims, the Shiites (SHEE–ites) and Sunnis (SOON–eez). Shiites and Sunnis differ in some of their beliefs. Five times a day, calls to prayer ring out from the Islamic churches, called **mosques.** All of Iraq's Muslims stop whatever they are doing and pray to God, called **Allah.**

About one-fifth of Iraq's people are *Kurds* rather than Arabs. Iraq's Kurds live in northeastern Iraq. The Kurds are Sunni Muslims, but they have their own culture and language. For many years they have wanted their own country, too. The Iraqi government has defeated the Kurds' attempts to become independent. The army has even used poison gas against the Kurds.

Two Million Kurds Fled From Iraq To Turkey In 1991

Women At Mosque Doorway In Karbala

Daniel Lainé/Corbis

Francoise de Mulder/Corbis

ADMIT ONE

City Life
And
Country
Life

ADMIT ONE

Cultivating
The Desert
In
Mesopotamia

David Lees/©Corbis

Most Iraqis live in cities. Some city neighborhoods have old buildings, while others have modern high-rises. Still other neighborhoods have narrow old streets and colorful open-air markets called *souks*. Many cities were badly damaged during the Gulf War. Iraq has always bought some of its food from other countries. Since the war, much of that supply has been cut off, and many city-dwellers have had little to eat.

Life in the Iraqi countryside has never been easy. Farming is difficult in this hot, dry land. Even so, farmers continue to work hard. Most Iraqi farmers live in villages. Many live in buildings made of sun-dried mud. In marshy areas, some people travel by boat and live in houses made from reeds.

Marsh
Arab Village
Near An
Nasiriyah

Souk Market In
Ruins Of
Karbala

Nik Wheeler/Corbis

Françoise de Mulder/Corbis

18

☆ Baghdad

Karbala •

MESOPOTAMIA

• An Nasiriyah

Nik Wheeler/Corbis

Downtown
Baghdad

Teacher
With Students In
Saddam
City

Baghdad☆ • Saddam City

• An Nasiriyah
Al Basrah •

Francoise de Mulder/Corbis

Schools And Language

University Of Baghdad

Nik Wheeler/Corbis

Iraqi boys and girls attend primary school from age six through age eleven. There they learn reading, writing, and other basic skills. They also learn about their religion. Many students go on to secondary school for three years. There they learn more math and science. Another three years of secondary school prepares some students for college or a training school.

Most of Iraq's people speak the country's official language, *Arabic*. Iraqi Arabic is one of many types of Arabic. Such different kinds of a language are called **dialects**. Written Arabic uses 29 curved letters to represent sounds. Iraq's Kurds speak their own Kurdish language.

Marsh Arab Children In Class Near An Nasiriyah

Sign With Arabic Letters Over Al Basrah Lemonade Stand

Nik Wheeler/Corbis

Francoise de Mulder/Corbis

21

Work

Construction Worker From Al Basrah

Nik Wheeler/Corbis

Iraqis work in many types of jobs. Some still work in the oil industry, despite damage from the recent wars. Many others raise food crops and herds of animals. Some people near rivers and marshes make their living harvesting fish. In recent years, the government has drained many of Iraq's marshes. Many marsh-dwellers have lost their jobs or left the country.

Other Iraqis are merchants who sell goods in stores and markets. Still others work in offices or in factories that make plastics, electronic equipment, and other products.

Nik Wheeler/Corbis

Iraqi Fashion Models From Baghdad

Young Shoeshiners In Al Basrah

Francoise de Mulder/Corbis

22

DORA POWER PLANT ■ ☆ Baghdad

MARSHES
Al Basrah ●

Man At
Control
Center Of
Dora
Power Plant

Francoise de Mulder/Corbis

Karbala Man
Selling
Turkeys

Tigris River
•Saddam City
Karbala•
•An Nasiriyah

Francoise de Mulder/Corbis

Food

The foods of Iraq are tasty and often spicy. Iraqis do not eat pork because pigs are thought to be unclean. Instead, they prefer lamb, chicken, and fish. Lamb is often combined with vegetables to make a spicy stew. Rice and bread are served with most meals. *Pita* is a flat, round bread that is hollow inside.

One well-known dish is *kebab*—spiced meat and vegetables grilled on a stick. Another favorite food is *masgouf*, a Tigris River fish. Masgouf is grilled on a stick and served with a spicy sauce. Tea is the most popular drink in Iraq. Also popular is coffee, which is made very strong, thick, and sweet. Dairy products are made from the milk of cattle, goats, camels, sheep, and even water buffalo!

Woman With Breakfast Near An Nasirayah

Nik Wheeler/Corbis

Market Vegetable Stall In Saddam City

Caroline Penn/Corbis

Marsh Arab Drinking Tea Near An Nasiriyah

Nik Wheeler/Corbis

The favorite sport of the Iraqi people is soccer. Also popular are horse racing, boxing, volleyball, weightlifting, and basketball. Quieter games are enjoyed, too—especially chess and backgammon.

The arts are popular in Iraq as well. People enjoy storytelling, dance, music, poetry and writing, and the theater. Many Iraqis are skilled at traditional crafts such as weaving and pottery-making. And visiting with friends and family is always a favorite pastime.

Horses And Spectators At Baghdad Racetrack

Dean Conger/Corbis

Taq Kisra Man Plays One-stringed Musical Instrument

Children At Play In Al Basrah

Nik Wheeler/Corbis

Francoise de Mulder/Corbis

Baghdad ☆
Taq Kisra ⚬
Al Basrah ●

Stadium Card
Display At
Police
Games
In Baghdad

Wedding In
Baghdad

☆ Baghdad
Babylon ∴
Al Basrah •

Holidays

Iraqis celebrate a number of religious and other holidays. Family events, especially weddings, are celebrated as well. One of the most important religious holidays is *Eid ul-Fitr.* This holiday takes place at the end of a holy month called *Ramadan* (RAH–mah–dahn). During the 30 days of Ramadan, Muslims eat and drink nothing (called **fasting**) from sunup to sundown. The end of Ramadan is a time for feasting, visiting, and gift-giving.

Iraq is a fascinating country with a long, proud history. Perhaps someday, when our countries are on better terms, you will be able to visit Iraq. Think how much fun it would be to meet Iraq's interesting people and see its ancient ruins, colorful markets, and beautiful buildings!

Soldier At Martyrs' Monument Celebration

Francoise de Mulder/Corbis

Moslem Women Pray In Baghdad Mosque

Francoise de Mulder/Corbis

Sunset On the River Euphrates At Al Basrah

Charles & Josette Lenars/Corbis

Detail Of Ceramic Art On Babylon Gate

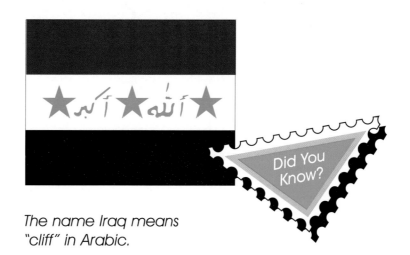

The name Iraq means "cliff" in Arabic.

Written Arabic is read from right to left—the opposite of English.

Even a dry country like Iraq can have problems with too much water. Sudden rains cause dangerous floods that happen quickly. These are called flash floods. When a flash flood happens in Iraq, it often destroys crops, washes out roads, and damages mud buildings.

Iraq's Sumerian community of long ago gave us many important inventions—including writing, the wheel, mathematics, and the calendar.

Iraq's city of Babylon was home to the Hanging Gardens of Babylon, one of the Seven Wonders of the Ancient World. These rooftop gardens were watered by a clever system of pumps.

HOW TO SAY IT

Hello	al-lahn wah sah-lahn
Goodbye	mah ahs-sah-leh-mah
Please	min fad-lak (to a man)
	min fad-lik (to a woman)
Thank You	shu-krahn
One	wah-hid
Two	it-neen
Three	tah-leh-tah
Yes	aye-wah
No	lah

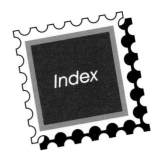

Allah (ALL–lah)
In the Islamic religion, Allah is the name for God. Iraqi Muslims pray to Allah five times a day.

continents (KON–tih–nents)
Continents are large areas of land mostly surrounded by water. Iraq lies at the edge of a large continent called Asia.

dialects (DIE–uh–lekts)
Dialects are local variations of a spoken language. English has many different dialects, and so does Arabic.

dictators (DIK–tay–ters)
Dictators are rulers who have total power over their people. Iraq's president, Saddam Hussein, rules the country as a dictator.

domesticated (doh–MESS–tih–kay–ted)
Domesticated plants and animals are raised by people instead of living in the wild. The people of ancient Mesopotamia domesticated many important food crops and animals.

fasting (FAST–ing)
Fasting is going without eating. During the holy month called Ramadan, Muslims fast every day from dawn to sunset.

irrigation (EER–ih–GAY–shun)
Irrigation is pumping river water onto dry farmland so crops can grow. Almost all of Iraq's crops need irrigation to survive.

Mesopotamia (MESS–uh–poh–TAY–mee–uh)
Mesopotamia is the ancient Greek name for central Iraq. It means "the land between the rivers" (the Tigris and Euphrates Rivers).

mosques (MOSKS)
Mosques are Islamic churches or temples. Many mosques are beautiful buildings with towers, rounded domes, and colorful decorations.

DATE DUE

FOLLETT